Bass Clef Music Manuscript Notat

By Randy McGravey

McGravey Music Manuscripts No. 9:
Bass Clef Music Manuscript Notation Paper

1st Edition
Created by Randy McGravey
Published through Amazon's *Kindle Direct Publishing*
Published 2017
Made in U.S.A.

For more information regarding educational opportunities, live performance, recording etc. visit
www.McGraveyMusic.com

Other publications by Randy McGravey:

The Guitar Techniques Handbook *...A Guide to Mastery of Tone*
The Guitar Techniques Handbook is designed to provide an in-depth understanding of different techniques that are available to guitarists. It is intended for intermediate guitarists and beyond who already have a moderate understanding of scales and basic chords. Proper use of this book will build up your arsenal of "tricks" and techniques which are audibly interesting and easy to play. With over 60 unique exercises, you are sure to combine and develop your own styles of playing, significantly increase playing speed, and become a more versatile player. Learn more than a dozen advanced guitar playing techniques including:

- Slurs
- Tapping
- Sweep Picking
- Harmonics
- Hybrid/chicken pickin'
- Fingerpicking... And much more!

Guitar Chords Complete
...A Complete Guide to Understanding and Playing Chords on Guitar
This book will teach you how to play virtually any chord on guitar. Not only will you learn basic shapes, but you will learn moveable chords and all of their variations, inversions and voicings. Learn how to play basic chords, jazz chords, altered chords, voice leading, substitutions, terminology, theory and much more. When done with this book, you will never need another chord book again, and you will be able to figure out anything that comes your way. The chord index in the back of the book also allows you to look up almost any chord. Go from a beginner to an expert of harmony in no time. Over 600 chords!

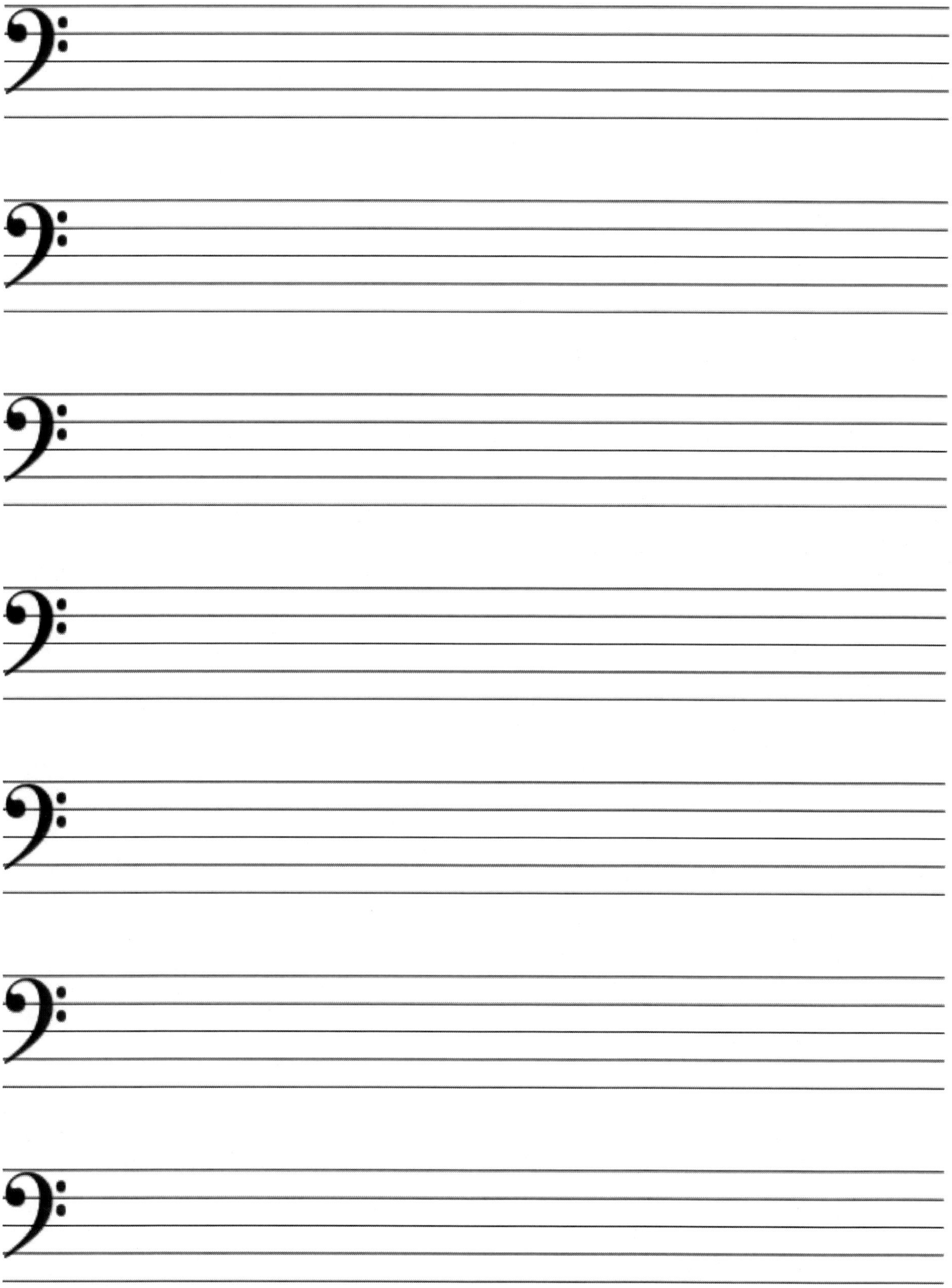

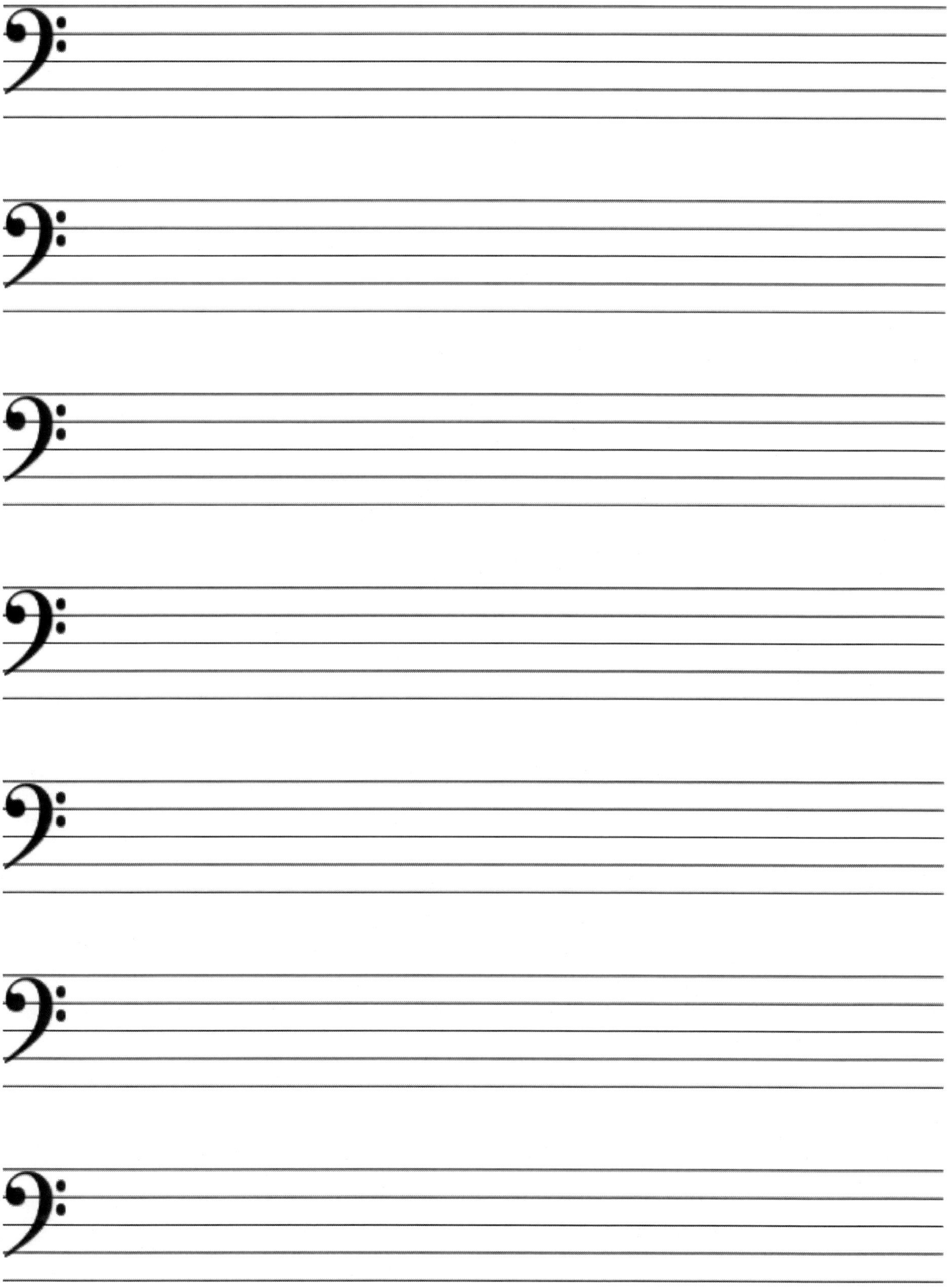

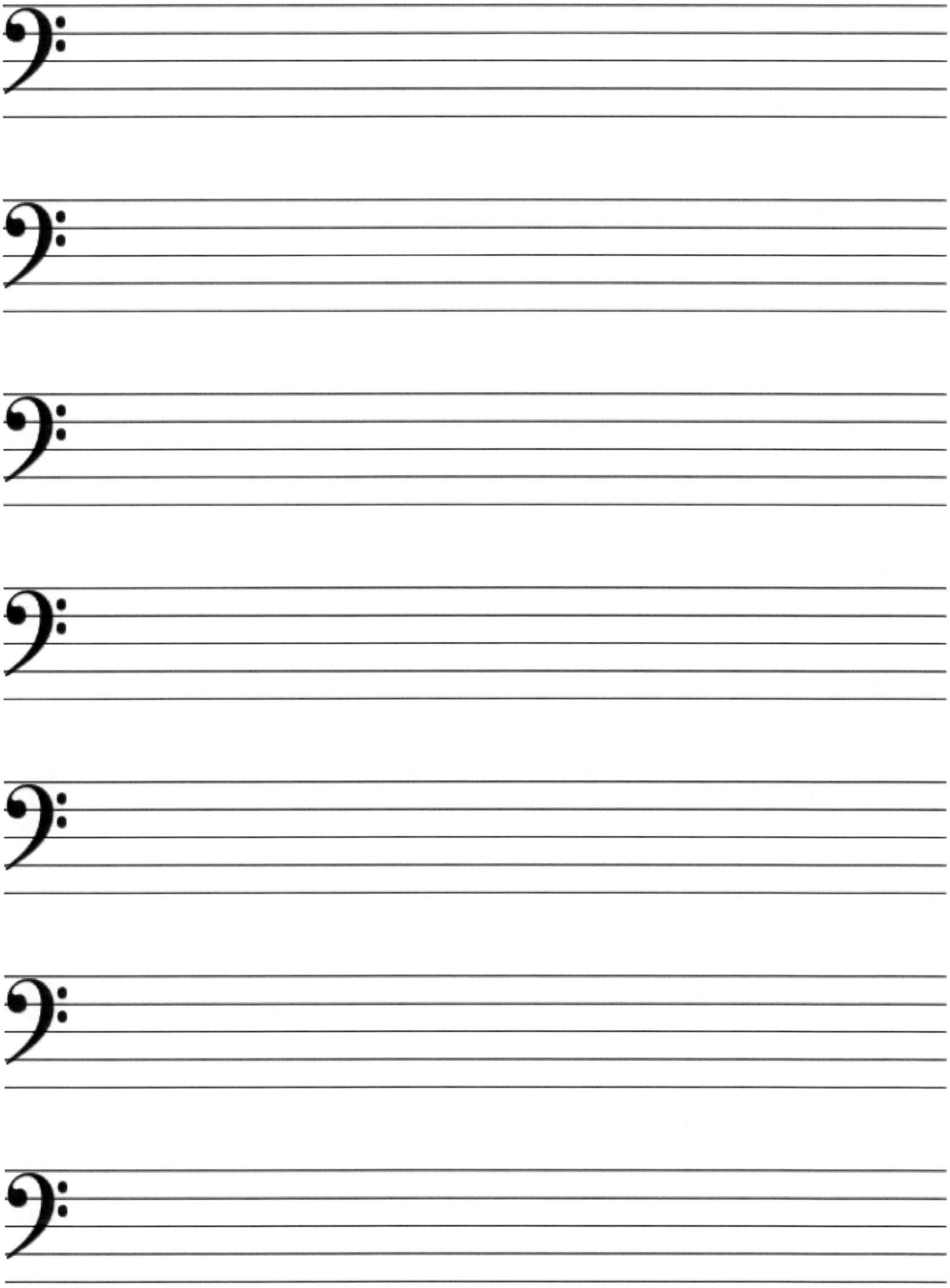

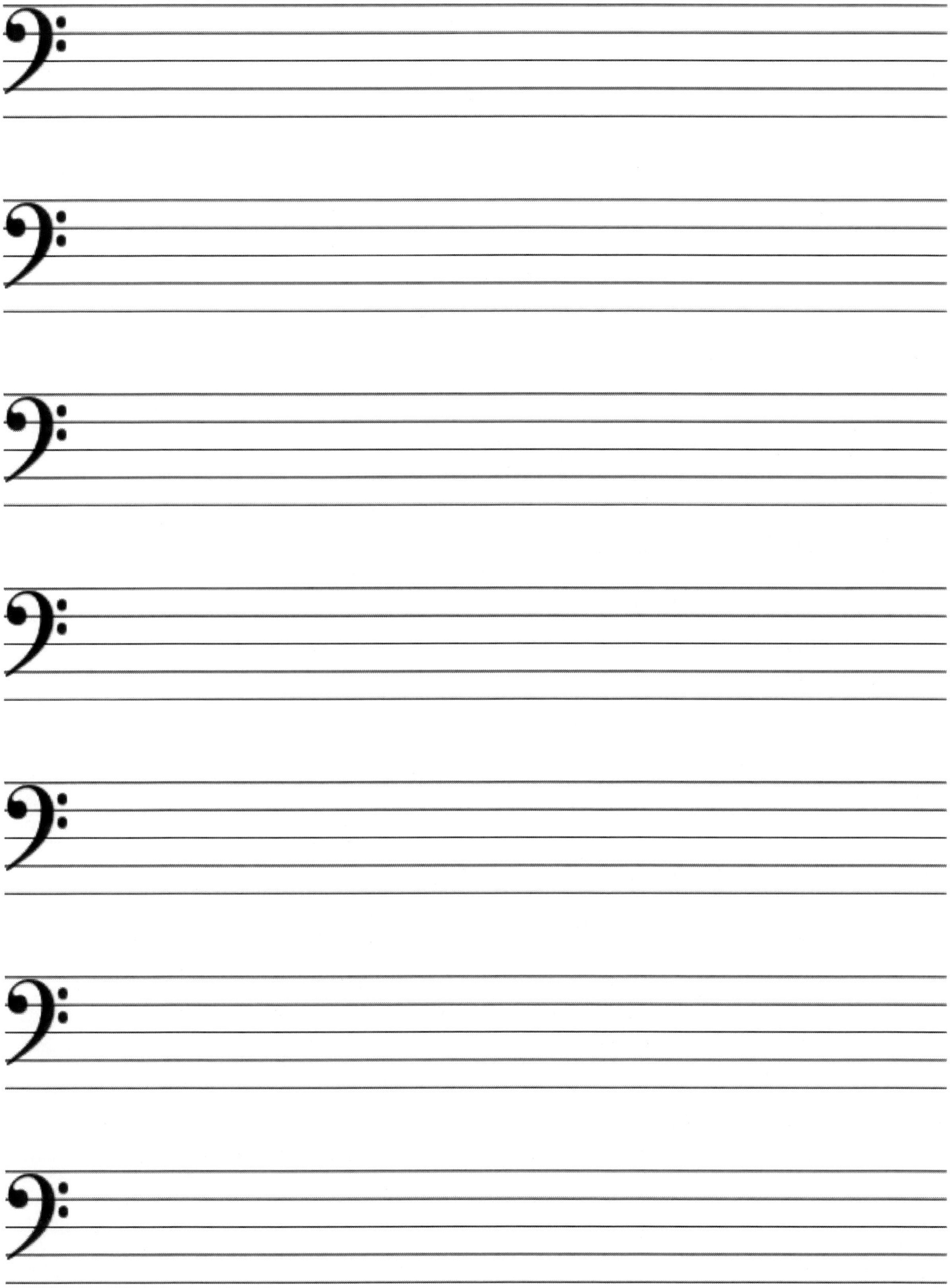

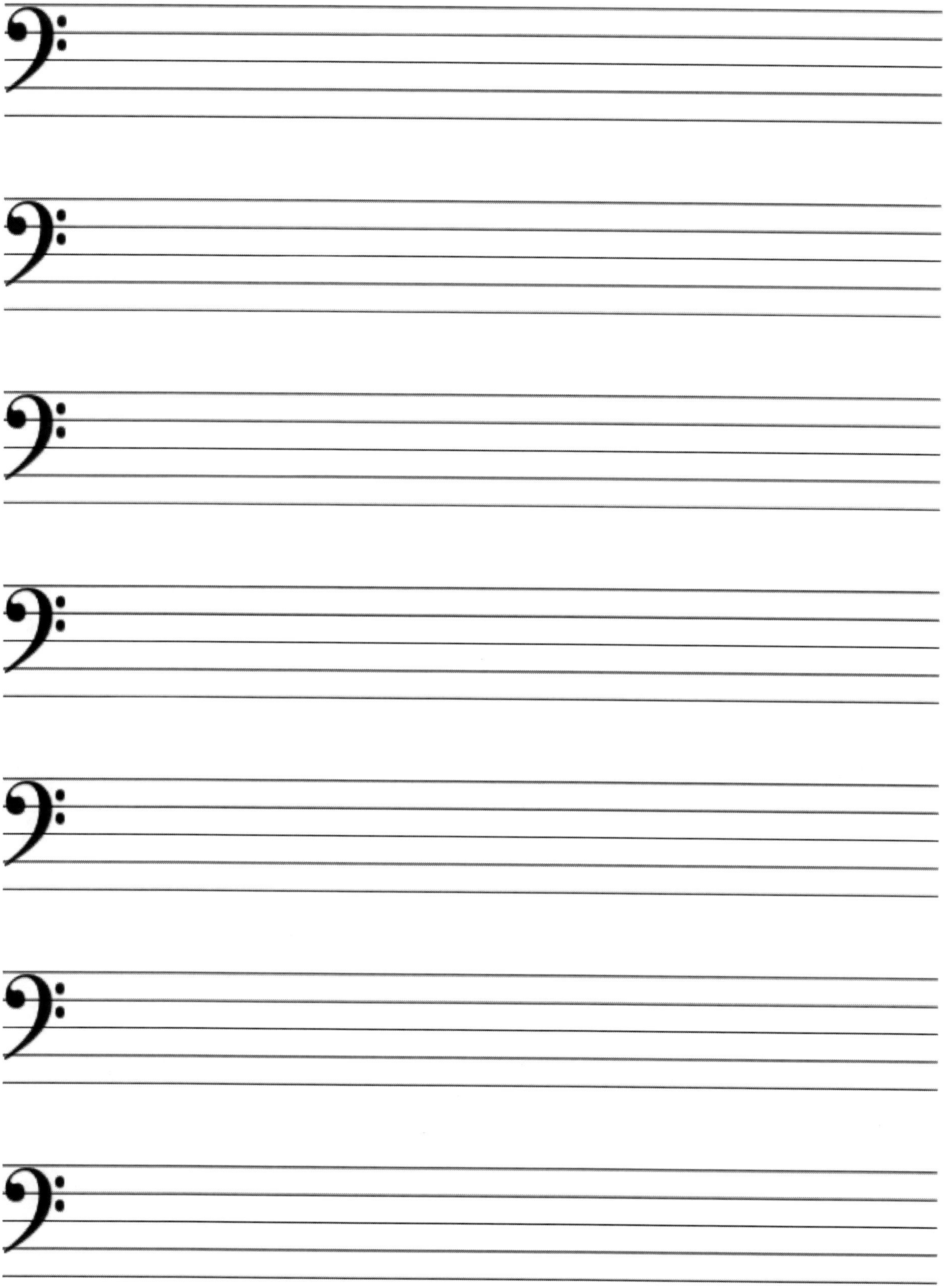

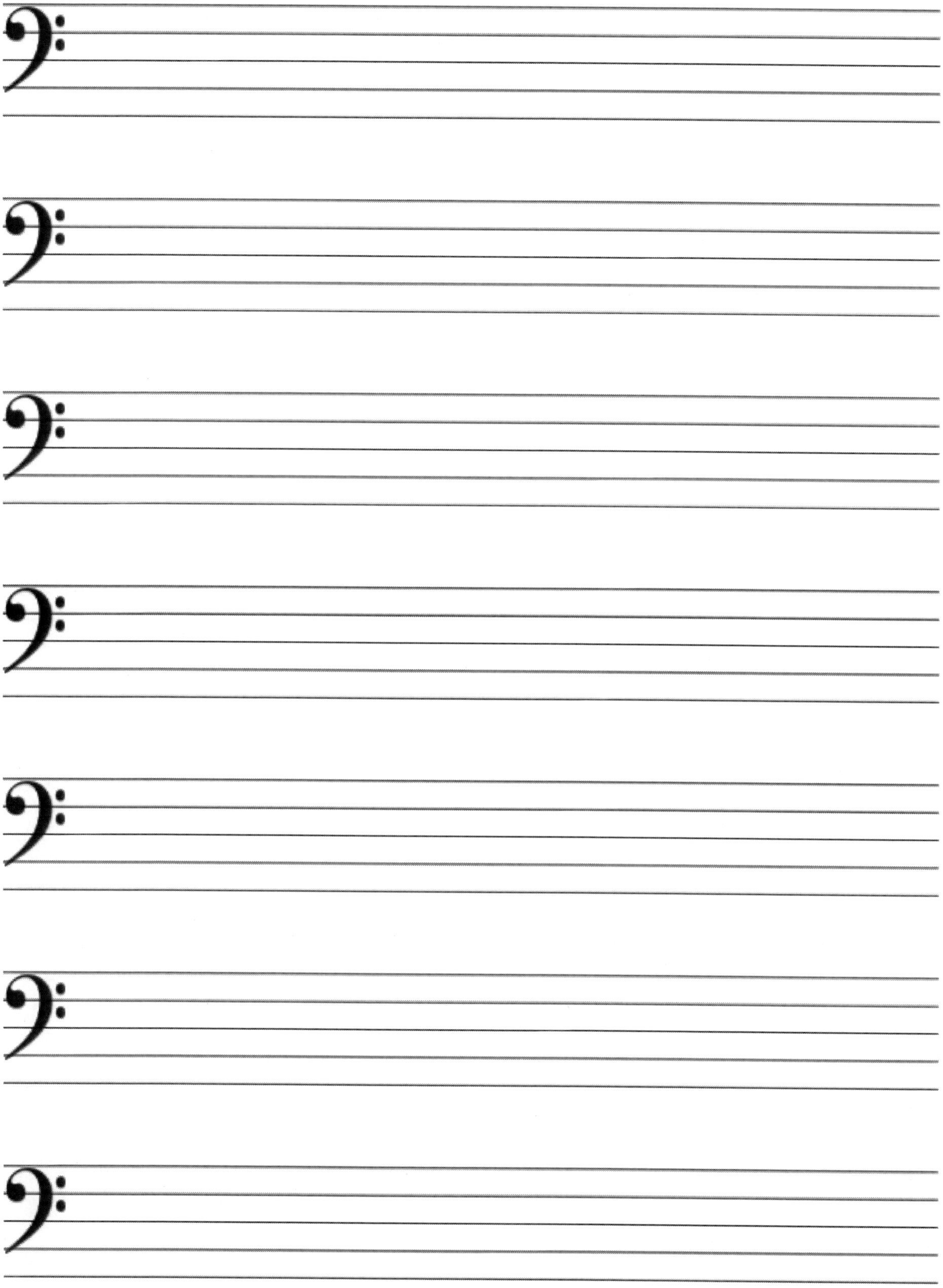

Made in United States
North Haven, CT
12 May 2023

36479306R10062